THE GREAT CRASH

1929, The Year the American Dream Fell

CATHERINE M. THORNE

Publisher's Note:

This book is not intended as a substitute for the financial or historical advice of a qualified professional. The author and publisher disclaim any liability arising directly or indirectly from the use of this book.

Disclaimer

No Financial or Investment Advice

This book is a historical narrative and analysis intended for educational and informational purposes only. It is not a source of financial, investment, or trading advice. The author and publisher are not financial advisors, brokers, or registered investment advisors. The information contained in this book should not be construed as a recommendation to buy, sell, or hold any security, investment, or asset, or to engage in any specific investment strategy.

Historical Analysis, Not Future Prediction

While this book examines the causes and consequences of the 1929 stock market crash, past performance and historical events are not reliable indicators of future results. The economic, regulatory, and market conditions of the present day are fundamentally different from those of the 1920s and 1930s. Any parallels drawn to modern markets are for illustrative and educational purposes only and should not be used as a basis for making financial decisions.

No Guarantee of Accuracy

Although the author and publisher have made every reasonable effort to ensure the accuracy and completeness of the information contained in this book, they assume no responsibility for any errors, omissions, or contrary interpretations of the subject matter. Historical records can be incomplete or conflicting, and new research may emerge that alters the understanding of these events. The author and publisher do not guarantee the accuracy, timeliness, or completeness of any information presented herein.

No Liability

The author and publisher shall not be held liable or responsible for any loss or damage allegedly caused, directly or indirectly, by the information or ideas contained, suggested, or referenced in this book. This includes, but is not limited to, financial losses, investment losses, or any other damages, personal or professional. The reader is solely responsible for their own financial decisions and actions.

Trademarks and Copyrights

All trademarks and copyrighted materials mentioned in this book are the property of their respective owners. Their use in this book is for educational, commentary, and illustrative purposes and does not imply endorsement or affiliation with the author or publisher.

TABLE OF CONTENT

Introduction

Black Thursday – The World Trembles

A low, nervous hum had filled the New York Stock Exchange at the opening bell, but by 11:00 a.m. on October 24, 1929, it had shattered into a sustained, visceral roar. The air, thick with the smell of sweat, fear, and cheap cigars, was electric with panic.

The ticker tape, that relentless, mechanical prophet of fortune, was falling hopelessly behind, its clattering voice drowned out by the bedlam. It was no longer reporting prices; it was delivering a eulogy, line by agonizing line.

Paper rained down like a blizzard of defeat. Sell orders—millions of them—piled up in a tidal wave of desperation. Where just weeks before there had been a euphoric, unshakable confidence, now there were only the contorted faces of men watching a century of American progress evaporate in a single morning.

A floor trader, his collar torn and eyes wide with disbelief, screamed himself hoarse, his voice lost in the cacophony. He was not just losing money; he was witnessing the unraveling of a fundamental truth—that stocks, like America itself, would only ever go up.

High above the fray, in a panelled office that seemed to exist in a different universe, the most powerful bankers in the world gathered in haste. Men like J.P. Morgan Jr., the son of a man who had once single-handedly halted a prior panic, now looked down upon a maelstrom their fathers would not have recognized. They spoke in low, urgent tones, their wealth a fortress that was suddenly, terrifyingly, under siege. They were there to stem the tide, but the ocean of panic was already breaching the walls.

Miles away, in a perfectly ordinary kitchen in Queens, a different kind of tragedy was playing out in silence. Arthur Miller, a shopkeeper who had invested his life's savings on the advice of his barber, stared at the newspaper left on his table.

The numbers on the page were abstract, but the cold dread in his stomach was not. The new car, the college fund for his daughter, the security he had worked for his entire life—it was all leaking away, minute by minute, with every delayed tick of a machine he had never seen. He was not a speculator; he was a believer in the new era, and his faith was being broken.

How did this happen? How did the soaring, seemingly unshakable prosperity of the "Roaring Twenties"—an age of radios, automobiles, and boundless optimism—lead to this cataclysm on the floor of the Exchange? The chaos of Black Thursday was not a beginning, but an ending. It was the violent, convulsive finale to a decade-long drama of greed, innovation, and delusion.

This is the story of the Great Crash. It is a forensic investigation into the causes and consequences of that collapse. It is a tale of the brilliant minds who believed they had conquered the business cycle, the everyday citizens who bet their futures on a dream, and the few voices of warning that were drowned out by the roar of the crowd.

To understand the fall, we must first return to the dizzying heights of the boom, to a time when it seemed the sky was the only limit.

Part I

The Roaring Twenties – The Illusion of Perpetual Prosperity

Chapter 1

A New Economic Era

The Great War was over, and in the weary but hopeful silence that followed, America drew a deep, ambitious breath. While Europe set about the grim task of burying its dead and rebuilding its shattered landscapes, the United States found itself in an unprecedented position: it was no longer a fledgling nation on the global stage, but its undisputed economic powerhouse.

The conflict had transformed the country from a debtor into the world's creditor, and a profound, buoyant optimism seeped into the national character.

This was more than just peace; it was a dawn, promising a future engineered not by generals and diplomats, but by industrialists and inventors.

This new era was built on a foundation of roaring factories and a cascade of technological marvels that began to reshape the very fabric of daily life. At the forefront was the automobile, and Henry Ford was its prophet.

His Model T was no longer a luxury for the elite; it was a tool of democratization, rolling off the assembly line in such staggering numbers that it put the nation on wheels.

Ford's genius was not merely in building cars, but in building them affordably, and in paying his workers a wage that allowed them to become his customers.

The car ceased to be a mere machine; it became a symbol of freedom, shrinking vast distances and fueling a new, restless mobility.

Simultaneously, other inventions were weaving a web of connectivity and convenience previously unimaginable. The radio, once a crackling toy for hobbyists, evolved into a central hearth of the American home. Through its static-tingled speaker flowed not just news and music, but a shared national culture.

Voices from New York and Chicago could now be heard in the farmhouses of Iowa and the bungalows of California, creating a collective experience that unified a dispersed populace. In the skies, Charles Lindbergh's daring solo flight across the Atlantic transformed aviation from a dangerous novelty into a symbol of heroic progress, hinting at a future where the skies themselves would be a new frontier for commerce.

And inside the home, a quiet revolution was underway as electric irons, vacuum cleaners, and refrigerators began to unshackle homemakers from the most burdensome of domestic labors, promising a life of modern ease.

This explosion of plenty could not have been sustained by mere desire; it required a new engine of commerce. That engine was modern advertising. No longer content to simply inform the public about a product's features, advertisers learned to sell aspiration.

They tapped into psychology, crafting campaigns that associated goods with social status, romantic success, and personal fulfillment. A car was not just transportation; it was an expression of virility and independence. A new radio was not just a device; it was your family's ticket to the wider world.

To bridge the gap between aspiration and reality, the financial innovation of installment buying—"buy now, pay later"—became the era's irresistible lubricant. This simple, seductive concept dismantled the old-fashioned virtue of saving up. Why wait for a refrigerator when, for a small down payment, you could have one today?

This system unleashed a torrent of consumer spending, fueling the economic boom but also quietly chaining millions to a web of monthly payments. It gave birth to a new social anxiety, perfectly captured by the popular cartoon strip, "Keeping Up with the Joneses."

The pressure was no longer merely to possess, but to possess *the latest*—to match your neighbor's new car, their radio cabinet, their electric washing machine, in a relentless and increasingly expensive pantomime of prosperity.

Thus, as the 1920s progressed, a powerful and intoxicating illusion took hold: that of perpetual prosperity. It seemed a new, frictionless form of capitalism had been born, a perfect machine where rising production was met with insatiable consumption, all funded by easy credit and fueled by boundless optimism.

The machine appeared so flawless, so self-sustaining, that few stopped to wonder what would happen if the fuel of confidence ever ran out.

Chapter 2

The Engine of the Boom

Beneath the glittering surface of the New Era, a complex and powerful engine was humming, driving the nation's prosperity to ever-greater heights.

This machine was not powered by a single invention, but by a new and intoxicating faith in scale, leverage, and perpetual growth. Its architects were the titans of industry and finance, men who saw not a national economy, but an empire to be built.

The most potent symbol of this new order was the rise of the giant corporation and, more dramatically, the public utility holding company.

Visionaries like Samuel Insull, a former assistant to Thomas Edison, did not simply build power companies; they constructed vast, pyramidal empires.

Through a labyrinth of holding companies stacked atop one another, Insull controlled a sprawling network of electric utilities that spanned dozens of states. The structure was a masterpiece of financial leverage.

A small investment at the top of the pyramid could control assets worth a hundred times its value. This magnified profits spectacularly during the good times, creating an illusion of unstoppable corporate genius and delivering massive returns to eager investors.

The utilities stocks became blue-chip darlings, their steady dividends seen as a sure bet in an ever-brightening, electrified world.

Yet, this faith in endless appreciation was not confined to Wall Street. A harbinger of the speculative mania to come erupted not in the canyons of Manhattan, but in the sun-baked marshes of Florida.

The Florida Land Boom of 1925 was a delirious preview of the coming crash. Fuelled by advertisements promising a tropical paradise, speculators descended on Miami and its surroundings, buying and selling parcels of land, often mere lots of swampland, with dizzying speed. Prices quadrupled and quintupled in months.

The goal was not to build homes, but to flip the paper contracts to a greater fool before the music stopped. And stop it did. A hurricane in 1926, coupled with railroad embargoes and the simple fact that the supply of "greater fools" was finite, collapsed the bubble almost overnight.

It was a stark, regional warning of how easily avarice could detach value from reality—a warning that was largely ignored by a nation focused on the seemingly more sophisticated markets of the North.

For all its roaring energy, the economic engine was running on faulty mechanics. While the stock ticker and the corporate report gleamed with health, foundational cracks were widening.

In the nation's heartland, American agriculture was in a state of quiet collapse. During the war, farmers had expanded production and taken on debt to feed Europe.

Now, with European fields restored and global demand slack, prices for wheat, cotton, and corn plummeted. Foreclosures swept through the Midwest, painting a grim picture of despair that stood in stark contrast to the urban euphoria.

This malaise was not isolated to the farms. While productivity soared in factories, the wages of the average industrial worker stagnated. The profits from the efficiency revolution flowed not to the factory floor, but to corporate coffers and into the pockets of shareholders.

The result was a dangerous and growing imbalance in the economy. The capacity to produce goods was outstripping the ability of the masses to consume them.

A small fraction of the population held a vastly disproportionate share of the wealth, and their money was increasingly funneled into speculative ventures rather than into the steady, broad-based consumer demand that truly sustains an economy.

The boom, therefore, was a paradox. It was both real and fragile. The technological advances and corporate expansions were genuine, but they were built upon a speculative frenzy and a consumer base whose foundations were crumbling.

The engine was racing, its pistons firing, but the fuel line was clogged, and the warning lights on the dashboard were beginning to blink red, unseen by drivers hurtling confidently into the night.

Chapter 3

Everybody Ought to Be Rich

A profound shift was occurring in the national psyche, one that moved the stock market from the wood-paneled smoking rooms of the elite to the bustling conversation of the everyday.

The great American pastime was no longer just baseball; it was speculation. The dizzying ascent of stock prices, splashed across the front pages of newspapers, created an irresistible siren song.

The market was no longer viewed as a risky arena for financiers, but as a guaranteed vehicle for wealth-building, a national lottery where it seemed every ticket was a winner. The phrase "Everybody Ought to Be Rich," popularized by financial evangelist John J. Raskob in a famous Ladies' Home Journal article, was not merely a suggestion; for millions, it became an article of faith.

This new dogma sparked the great democratization of the market. The small investor—the shopkeeper, the clerk, the schoolteacher—now elbowed their way onto the trading floor, figuratively speaking.

They didn't need the gilded credentials of a Morgan partner to participate. All that was required was a little cash for the margin and a boundless optimism. Brokers' offices, once sober and exclusive establishments, popped up in every city and town, becoming vibrant, chaotic hubs where anyone could watch the flickering ticker tape and dream.

The intoxicating power of margin buying meant that a schoolteacher could control a thousand dollars of stock with only a hundred of her own.

Her gains, on paper, were magnified tenfold, creating a feedback loop of euphoria and further investment.

This new culture of speculation bred its own folklore. Anecdotes became legend, passed along in barbershops and on factory floors like gospel. The story of the barber in Cleveland who parlayed a few hundred dollars into a small fortune by following a tip on Radio Corporation of America (RCA). The tale of the chauffeur who, by eavesdropping on his wealthy passengers' conversations, amassed a portfolio that rivaled his employer's.

These stories, whether entirely true or generously embellished, served a critical purpose: they eroded caution and validated the belief that the old rules of hard work and slow saving were obsolete. Genius was no longer required; all one needed was the nerve to get in the game.

Feeding this hunger was a media ecosystem all too eager to fuel the mania. Respected newspapers like the *New York Times* ran bullish forecasts from esteemed economists, while their financial pages chronicled the daily triumphs of the market. But more influential still were the outright cheerleaders and the shadowy world of "tipster sheets." Publications and self-proclaimed oracles promised inside information and guaranteed gains for a subscription fee.

They peddled rumors as analysis and hope as strategy, creating a constant buzz of "can't-miss" opportunities. The line between financial journalism and promotional hype became dangerously blurred, creating an echo chamber where the only voice worth hearing was the one that promised more.

Thus, a self-perpetuating cycle was born. The small investor, empowered by margin and enticed by the media, jumped in, driving prices higher. Those rising prices created more success stories, which in turn drew in more investors. It was a financial fever dream, a collective conviction that a new, frictionless form of wealth had been discovered.

In this atmosphere, the very concept of risk was ridiculed as the timid philosophy of a bygone age. The market, it was widely believed, had achieved a permanently high plateau, and the only real danger was being left behind.

Part II

The Fever Dream – The Speculative Orgy

Chapter 4

The Mechanics of Mania

The soaring market of the late 1920s was not built on a foundation of solid cash, but on a towering and precarious structure of credit. The entire speculative edifice rested on a single, intoxicating mechanism: the margin loan. To understand the frenzy that followed, one must first understand this simple, yet devastatingly powerful, financial instrument.

In essence, buying on margin was placing a small down payment on a stock, and borrowing the rest of the money from a stockbroker. If a share of General Electric cost $100, an investor didn't need to save the full amount.

He could purchase it with just $10 of his own money, and borrow the remaining $90 from the broker. This leverage was the rocket fuel of the bull market. A 10% rise in the stock's price to $110 meant the investor's own $10 stake had doubled. He could sell, repay the $90 loan, and walk away with $20—a 100% return on his initial investment. It was financial alchemy, and it created a nation of instant geniuses.

But this magic had a dark, unforgiving flip side. The loan from the broker was secured by the purchased stock itself. Should the stock's price fall, the value of that collateral shrank. If it dropped to $85, the investor's initial $10 was now almost entirely wiped out.

At this point, the broker would issue a dreaded "margin call," demanding the investor immediately deposit more cash to restore the collateral. If the investor couldn't pay—and most small-time speculators had poured every spare dollar into the market—the broker would ruthlessly sell the stock out from under him to recoup the loan. This forced selling, happening en masse, could turn a modest market dip into a cascading avalanche.

This system of margin buying was itself built upon another, larger credit structure: brokers' loans. Where did the brokers get the billions of dollars to lend to their eager clients? They borrowed it themselves, from banks, corporations, and even individual investors, who found the high, short-term interest rates on these loans to be a safe and profitable haven for their cash.

This created an inverted pyramid of debt. At the top were the stocks, their prices inflated by margin buying. Beneath them were the billions in brokers' loans propping those prices up. This was the house of cards: stable only as long as the value of the stocks at the top continued to rise.

Any sustained decline would force margin calls, trigger forced selling, and threaten the entire chain of credit with collapse.

Adding another layer of complexity and risk was the meteoric rise of the investment trust, the era's version of a mutual fund. These companies pooled money from thousands of small investors and used it to buy a diversified portfolio of stocks. In theory, this was a sound idea, offering the little guy access to professional management and diversification. In practice, the trusts became speculative monsters in their own right.

Many trusts were highly leveraged, buying stocks on margin just like their clients. Worse, they were often labyrinthine in their structure. A "parent" trust would create a "child" trust, investing in its shares, and that child might then create another.

This pyramid scheme of ownership created incredible opacity. An investor buying a share in a top-tier trust had no real idea what assets they ultimately owned, as the value was filtered through multiple layers of holding companies.

The trusts also engaged in cross-holdings, buying large blocks of each other's shares, artificially inflating their apparent value in a closed loop of speculation. They weren't just betting on the market; they *were* the market, and their complex, interwoven nature meant that if one faltered, it could pull a dozen others down with it.

Together, these three elements—margin buying, brokers' loans, and investment trusts—formed the intricate and highly combustible engine of the mania. They created a world where real value was obscured by borrowed money and dizzying complexity, a world where everyone was a winner, so long as the music never stopped.

Chapter 5

The Voices of Caution and the Cult of Optimism

As the speculative fever reached its peak in the summer of 1929, a dissonant chord began to sound, faint at first, but growing increasingly persistent. It was the voice of caution, and in the roaring chorus of the bull market, it was treated not as sober counsel, but as heresy.

The most prominent prophet of doom was an eccentric, Massachusetts-based statistician named Roger Babson. A man of peculiar habits and unshakable conviction, Babson had long preached a gospel of market cycles, insisting that what goes up must, by the immutable laws of physics and economics, come down. While crowds hung on every bullish pronouncement, Babson delivered a speech at a National Business Conference in September that sent a shiver through the financial world. "Sooner or later," he declared with grim certainty, "a crash is coming, and it may be terrific."

He pointed to the rampant speculation, the unsustainable leverage, and the simple mathematical fact that trees do not grow to the sky. The wire services picked up his words, and the market, jittery for a moment, experienced a sharp, sudden sell-off that was quickly dubbed the "Babson Break." The establishment rushed to dismiss him as a broken record, a perennial pessimist finally being noticed only because of the scale of the boom he criticized.

The most powerful of these dismissals came from the heart of the academic and financial elite. Irving

Fisher, a celebrated Yale economist and one of the most famous financial minds in the world, became the high priest of the New Era faith.

A man who had himself made a fortune by inventing the Rolodex-like "Index Visible" filing system, Fisher embodied the marriage of intellectual authority and market success. He had developed complex mathematical models that, to him, proved the market was not overvalued but was correctly pricing in the dazzling future profits of American corporations.

As stocks wobbled after Babson's warning, Fisher delivered the reassurance a nervous public craved. In early October, he made his immortal declaration to a group of bankers: "Stock prices have reached what looks like a permanently high plateau."

Fisher was not a charlatan; he was a true believer, a captive of his own elegant theories. His immense authority provided the intellectual cover that allowed millions to ignore their gnawing doubts. If a genius like Fisher said it was safe, who was a mere shopkeeper or clerk to question him?

His confidence became a self-fulfilling prophecy for a few more weeks, a dam holding back a rising tide of anxiety.

Lending the full weight of the presidency to this cult of optimism was Herbert Hoover. Having taken office in March 1929, he was a man steeped in a profound belief in progress, efficiency, and the fundamental soundness of the American economic system.

He had tirelessly championed the new, "scientific" approach to economics that promised an end to the brutal boom-bust cycles of the past. From the White House came a steady stream of statements affirming the nation's "boundless prosperity" and the "healthy and optimistic" state of business.

This was not merely public relations; it was an article of Hoover's deeply held faith. To suggest the system was fundamentally flawed was to challenge the very core of American exceptionalism.

Thus, by the autumn of 1929, a stark battle of narratives was underway. On one side stood the lonely voices of caution like Babson, pointing to the structural cracks in the foundation. On the other stood a powerful alliance of academic celebrity, presidential authority, and Wall Street interest, all preaching a gospel of perpetual growth.

The public, their pockets lined with paper profits and their minds clouded by the intoxicating rhetoric of the New Era, knew whom they wanted to believe. They chose the promise of the plateau over the prophecy of the precipice. The stage was set not for a slow awakening, but for a shattering disillusionment.

Chapter 6

The Peak and the First Cracks

The air in September 1929 was thick with a triumphant, almost delirious, certainty. On the third day of the month, the Dow Jones Industrial Average climbed to a closing high of 381.17. It was the summit of the mountain, the culmination of a near-decade-long ascent.

From the ticker tape parlors to the editorial boards of the nation's newspapers, the mood was one of self-congratulation. The prophets of the New Era, it seemed, had been right all along.

The old laws of economics had been suspended, and this plateau of prosperity was indeed permanent.

But summits are precarious places, where the air is thin and the view can be deceptive. The very height of the peak meant there was only one direction left to go. The first gust of wind came from a familiar, and until then, largely ignored, source.

On September 5, at the National Business Conference, Roger Babson reiterated his grim prophecy. "The crash is coming," he stated plainly, "and it may be terrific." He had said it before, but this time, the market, perhaps made nervous by its own altitude, listened.

The reaction was swift and brutal. In the final hour of trading, a massive sell-order hit the market, triggering a chain reaction of automated stop-losses and fearful liquidations. The Dow plunged, erasing billions in paper wealth in a matter of minutes. The financial press, scrambling to name the sudden tremor, dubbed it the "Babson Break."

The established powers rushed to calm the waters. Irving Fisher dismissed the drop as a "shaking out of the lunatic fringe," and Charles E. Mitchell, a prominent banker, declared that the "markets were now in a healthy condition." The slide was temporarily halted, their authority propping up the collective faith.

Yet, the spell had been broken. The Babson Break was a hairline fracture in the foundation of the bull market. Throughout the rest of September and into a volatile October, the market failed to recapture its serene confidence. It moved in fits and starts—a few days of hopeful recovery followed by another shudder of selling. The movements were not yet a collapse, but they were no longer an ascent. The smooth, upward trajectory was replaced by a jagged, nervous line on the chart.

In brokerage houses across the country, the mood began to shift from euphoria to anxiety. The initial, thrilling margin calls—requests for more cash to cover declining stock values—had been met with ease by investors flush with paper profits.

But as the declines continued, the calls became more frequent and more insistent. The circular logic of the boom was reversing itself. Falling prices triggered margin calls, which forced investors to sell shares to cover them, which drove prices down further, triggering more margin calls. It was a vicious, self-feeding cycle, and the sound of its grinding machinery began to echo through the financial district.

A palpable tension settled over Wall Street. The newspapers still carried bullish statements, but the headlines grew more tentative. The whispers in the brokers' offices were no longer about which stock would double next, but about who had been wiped out in the last dip. The unshakeable faith was now shaken.

The market was no longer a one-way bet; it was a battlefield, and the first, faint smell of panic was carried on the autumn wind. The permanently high plateau was beginning to crumble at the edges, and the ground was starting to tremble.

Part III

The Crash – The Deluge

Chapter 7

Black Thursday (October 24)

The tension that had been coiling for weeks finally snapped on the morning of Thursday, October 24th. From the moment the gavel fell at the New York Stock Exchange, there was no preamble, no slow build. The market went straight over a cliff. A torrent of sell orders, pent up from days of fear and margin calls, flooded the trading floor simultaneously from across the country. The ticker tape, that steady pulse of the market, instantly fell behind, its frantic clatter a useless echo of transactions that had already happened at plummeting prices.

On the floor, the scene devolved into a surreal tableau of panic. The roar was no longer that of commerce, but of a mob trapped in a burning building. Well-dressed men, their faces contorted in terror, shoved and shouted, their paper collars wilted with sweat, their eyes fixed on the giant chalkboards where quotes were scrawled, each new number a deeper cut. Here and there, a trader would simply collapse, overcome by the sight of his ruin, to be dragged to the sidelines.

By 11:00 a.m., the market was in free fall. Blue-chip stocks like U.S. Steel and General Electric were being dumped for losses of thirty, forty, fifty points. There were no buyers, only sellers, and the prices became a grotesque auction of despair.

In brokerage offices from Main Street to Wall Street, crowds gathered around the translucent ticker displays, their cheers and laughter from weeks before replaced by a suffocating silence, broken only by gasps and occasional sobs as they watched their futures vanish in the unspooling tape. The world was witnessing the first great financial heart attack of the modern age.

In a last, desperate bid to stop the hemorrhage, a secret meeting was convened at noon at the offices of J.P. Morgan & Co., directly across the street from the Exchange. The most powerful financiers of the age—including the heads of National City Bank, Chase National Bank, and Guaranty Trust— gathered in the same room where J.P. Morgan the elder had halted the Panic of 1907.

They were the so-called "Bankers' Pool." Recognizing that psychology, not economics, was now in control, they made a monumental decision. They would pour a massive pool of capital—some $240 million—into the market to buy key stocks and project an image of unshakable confidence.

At 1:30 p.m., Richard Whitney, the vice-president of the Exchange and the broker for the Morgan bank, strode onto the chaotic floor. He moved with theatrical calm, a bastion of order in the storm.

He walked directly to the U.S. Steel post and, in a loud, clear voice, placed a bid for 25,000 shares at a price well above the current market. He then moved to other pivotal posts, doing the same for other blue-chip stocks. The effect was electric.

The gesture was a powerful signal: the titans of finance were stepping in. The money was a tourniquet, but the message was the real medicine. The bleeding slowed. A rally, fierce and hopeful, exploded in the final hour.

When the closing bell rang, the market had recovered a significant portion of its catastrophic losses. The bankers were hailed as heroes. Newspapers, desperate for a positive spin, declared the crisis over, the panic contained. But it was a mirage.

The stability was an illusion, purchased with a finite pool of capital and a powerful bluff. The underlying sickness—the mountain of margin debt, the shattered confidence of the small investor, the fundamental disconnect between price and value—remained. The bankers had calmed the patient, but the fever still raged. The deluge had been paused, not stopped.

Chapter 8

The Terrible Tuesday-October 29

The fragile calm of the weekend shattered on Monday, October 28th. The reassurance offered by the bankers' pool evaporated as a new, more profound wave of selling crashed over the market. The Dow plummeted another 13%. The stage was now set for the main event, a day of such unparalleled financial destruction that it would sear itself into history as Black Tuesday.

October 29, 1929, did not begin with panic, but with a grim, resigned certainty. The dam of confidence had not just cracked; it had vaporized. From the opening bell, a tidal wave of sell orders from every corner of the nation hit the trading floor. There was no longer any thought of buying for a bargain; the sole, desperate impulse was to escape. The machinery of the market, designed for orderly trading, simply broke under the strain.

A record-shattering 16.4 million shares would change hands, a volume so immense the ticker tape fell hours behind, rendering it a useless, lagging chronicle of a catastrophe that had already happened.

On the floor, traders were no longer shouting; they were screaming into a void, their voices raw, their faces masks of pure horror as they fought to execute orders at any price. By noon, the blue-chip stocks that Richard Whitney had propped up just days before were in freefall, losing decades of accumulated value in a single morning.

The ruin was absolute and democratized. In the opulent smoking rooms of private clubs, men of immense fortune sat in stunned silence, watching generational wealth evaporate. The legendary investor Jesse Livermore, who had famously shorted the panic of 1907, was now caught on the wrong side and faced staggering losses. But the true tragedy unfolded far from Wall Street.

In countless middle-class homes, families gathered around their radios, listening to the frantic news reports. The shopkeeper who had leveraged his business, the teacher who had invested her nest egg, the farmer who had bet on the boom—they all received their margin calls not as a request, but as a final verdict. Their life savings, built on the promise of a New Era, were wiped out before the ticker tape had even finished printing the opening trades.

From this cauldron of despair, a dark and enduring myth was born: the Wall Street window-jumper. Tales spread of ruined speculators leaping from skyscrapers to their deaths. While the suicide rate did increase in the aftermath, the image of a rain of bodies from financial district windows was a powerful exaggeration, a macabre folklore that perfectly captured the sense of a world plunging into the abyss. It was a metaphor made literal in the public imagination. The crash was not merely a financial event; it was an existential one.

The unshakable American faith in progress, prosperity, and the infallibility of its financial system had not just stumbled; it had jumped from a great height, and on Black Tuesday, it finally hit the ground.

Chapter 9

The Aftermath and the Slide

The closing bell on Black Tuesday did not mark an end, but a beginning. The spectacular, five-day collapse that culminated on October 29th was merely the detonation. What followed was a relentless, grinding decline that stretched through November and beyond, a slow-motion unraveling that systematically dismantled any remaining hope.

The crash was not a single storm, but the start of a financial ice age.

In the days and weeks following Black Tuesday, the market continued its sickening descent. The dramatic plunges of late October gave way to a steadier, more insistent decay. There were no more heroic rallies, no desperate consortia of bankers. Each small, temporary gain was met with a fresh wave of selling from investors who had been clinging to the wreckage, finally accepting their losses.

The Dow Jones, which had peaked at 381 in September, was like a ship slipping beneath the waves, descending to 198 by mid-November—a loss of nearly half its value in a matter of weeks. The air had gone out of the bubble, and the market was collapsing under its own weight.

The myth of the "organized support" was fully exposed. The Bankers' Pool, which had seemed so powerful on Black Thursday, was revealed to be a futile gesture against the sheer, impersonal force of a deleveraging market. The bankers' $240 million, a colossal sum in its own right, was a pebble thrown into a tsunami.

They had attempted to stand in the path of millions of margin calls, a global loss of confidence, and the structural flaws of the entire credit-driven system. Their funds were quickly swallowed by the selling pressure, and their credibility, the most potent part of their intervention, was utterly spent.

The lesson was stark: no individual or group, no matter how wealthy, could arrest the fundamental laws of economics once they had been set in motion.

The scale of the destruction was almost incomprehensible. By the time the market found a temporary bottom in mid-November, over $30 billion in wealth had been obliterated.

To a nation that had spent a decade in prosperity, this figure was an abstraction of terrifying magnitude. Journalists and politicians made it concrete: this was a sum greater than the total cost of World War I to the United States.

The entire financial burden of the nation's last great national trial—the ships, the shells, the soldiers' pay—had been wiped out in a few weeks on the stock ticker. It was more than money; it was faith, security, and the promise of the future, all gone. The Roaring Twenties were over, and the long, cold winter of the Great Depression had begun.

Part IV

The Reckoning – Causes and Consequences

Chapter 10

The Root Causes: A Perfect Storm

In the bleak aftermath of the crash, a single, haunting question demanded an answer: why? The collapse was too vast, too systemic, to be blamed on a single day of panic or a handful of foolish investors.

The truth was that the Great Crash was not caused by one failure, but by the convergence of several, each amplifying the others in a catastrophic symphony. It was the result of a perfect storm, brewing for a decade, that finally made landfall on Wall Street.

1. The Tinder: Over-speculation and the Margin System

The immediate trigger was the speculative orgy fueled by the margin system. This was the chemical that turned a healthy market into an inferno. By allowing investors to control vast amounts of stock with minimal capital, margin buying detached prices from reality and created a market built on debt, not value.

When prices began to falter, the system's built-in vicious cycle took over: falling prices triggered margin calls, which forced sell-offs, which drove prices down further. It was a financial doomsday machine, and in October 1929, it reached critical mass.

2. The Weak Foundation: A Fragile Banking System

Beneath the speculative frenzy lay a deeply flawed

American banking system. The nation was dotted with thousands of small, undercapitalized "unit banks," often tied to the fortunes of a single local industry or crop. These institutions were not only vulnerable to economic shocks but were also deeply enmeshed in the speculation, having lent billions to brokers for margin loans.

When the crash hit and these loans went bad, and as their own depositors rushed to withdraw savings, these banks had nowhere to turn. They folded by the hundreds, wiping out life savings and strangling the credit that businesses needed to survive, turning a stock market crash into a full-blown banking crisis.

3. The Structural Flaws: Unsound Economic Fundamentals

For all its glitter, the prosperity of the 1920s was profoundly uneven. While productivity soared, the fruits of this growth were concentrated in the hands of the wealthiest Americans. The vast majority of workers and farmers saw their incomes stagnate. This created a fundamental weakness: the economy's capacity to produce goods had outpaced the public's capacity to consume them.

Factories were churning out automobiles and appliances that fewer and fewer people could actually afford. The agricultural sector, which had never recovered from the post-war slump, was a disaster zone, leaving a quarter of the population with little purchasing power. The boom was built on a weak and narrowing base.

4. The Global Chain Reaction: A World Out of Balance

The storm was not confined to American shores. The international financial system, still reeling from World War I, was a web of instability. European nations, particularly Germany, were crippled by war debts and reparations, relying on American loans to stay afloat. The U.S. Smoot-Hawley Tariff Act of 1930 would later exacerbate this, but the protectionist sentiment was already rising, strangling global trade.

When American capital dried up after the crash and U.S. banks began calling in foreign loans to cover their domestic losses, the entire fragile structure collapsed, pulling the global economy down with it.

5. The Failed Helmsman: Poor Government Policy

Ultimately, the stewards of the economy failed to steer the ship away from the iceberg. The Federal Reserve, tasked with maintaining stability, committed a fatal two-part error. First, it kept interest rates low for too long during the boom, fueling the speculative fire. Then, when the crisis hit, it inexplicably tightened credit, raising rates and failing to act as a "lender of last resort" to provide liquidity to desperate banks. This catastrophic misjudgment transformed a market correction into a deep depression by allowing the money supply to collapse and the banking system to fail.

Individually, any one of these factors would have caused a recession. Combined, they created a vortex of economic destruction from which there would be no quick escape. The crash was not the cause of the Great Depression, but the spectacular symptom of a disease that had already infected the entire body economicarman

Chapter 11

The Human Toll

Behind the staggering statistics—the $30 billion vanished, the millions of shares traded—lay a reality the numbers could never capture: the profound, intimate human devastation that seeped into every city, every small town, and every home. The Crash was not an event that happened to the market; it was a catastrophe that happened to people, leaving a scar on the national psyche that would last for generations.

The first and most visible impact was the swift collapse of the world of work. Businesses that had expanded on credit saw their financing vanish overnight. Orders were canceled, factories fell silent, and payrolls were slashed.

The unemployment rate, a mere 3.2% in 1929, began its grim ascent, leaving one in four Americans without a job within three years. But for those who lived it, this was not a percentage point; it was the daily, humiliating ritual of the breadline. It was the sight of formerly proud, suited men standing in souplines, their heads bowed, their hands empty.

It was the engineer now selling apples on the street corner, the salesman taking any menial job he could find, the collective skills and ambitions of a nation suddenly rendered worthless.

For the middle class, the loss was less public but no less devastating. The life savings meticulously built over a lifetime—often poured into what were considered "safe" blue-chip stocks or held in a local bank—evaporated without a trace. The margin calls that wiped out speculators were matched by the bank failures that wiped out depositors; when a bank closed its doors, the savings within were often gone forever.

This led to the most visceral loss of all: the home. With no income and no savings, mortgage payments became impossible. Families across the country faced eviction, their furniture piled on the sidewalk, their futures suddenly homeless. The American Dream of stability and upward mobility was replaced by the stark reality of dispossession and rootlessness.

Perhaps the deepest wound was psychological. The Crash shattered the foundational American belief in progress and the promise that hard work guaranteed security. A pervasive sense of shame settled over the unemployed, who internalized their failure in a society that preached rugged individualism. The despair was palpable, a heavy blanket smothering the optimism of the previous decade.

Men who had been providers now felt like failures in their own homes; the confidence that had fueled the Roaring Twenties curdled into a deep-seated anxiety and a distrust of institutions—of banks, of corporations, and of the government itself.

The nation's spirit, once soaring, was now earthbound and broken. The collective trauma of seeing a seemingly solid world dissolve into chaos created a generation defined by caution, thrift, and an unshakable fear of financial risk.

The Great Crash had ended more than just a bull market; it had ended an era of innocence, replacing it with a new, harsh understanding of life's fragility in the modern economic age.

Chapter 12

The Government Responds

As the dust of the crash settled and the grim reality of a faltering economy set in, the nation instinctively turned its eyes to Washington. The man in the White House, Herbert Hoover, was not a passive bystander.

He was a brilliant engineer, a man of deep compassion forged by his global humanitarian work, and he believed fervently in the power of rational, voluntary action. His response, however, would become a masterclass in the collision of principled ideology and unprecedented crisis.

Hoover's guiding philosophy was "rugged individualism." He held an almost Jeffersonian faith in local communities, private charity, and the moral fortitude of American citizens and businesses to solve their own problems. He believed that direct federal relief would create a culture of dependency, crippling the very spirit of self-reliance that built the nation.

Instead of launching a large-scale government program, he embarked on a campaign of vigorous persuasion. He summoned business leaders to the White House, urging them to maintain wages and continue investment. He called upon governors and mayors to accelerate public works projects, and he asked the American people to give generously to local charities.

For Hoover, the depression was a temporary "liquidation" that required not a federal takeover, but a collective, voluntary tightening of belts and a reaffirmation of community spirit.

This philosophy hardened into catastrophic policy with the **Smoot-Hawley Tariff Act of 1930**. Intended to protect struggling American farmers and manufacturers from foreign competition, the act raised U.S. tariffs on over 20,000 imported goods to historic levels. It was an act of profound economic isolationism.

The reaction from America's trading partners was swift and retaliatory. Dozens of countries erected their own punishing tariffs against U.S. goods. World trade, already weakened by the financial panic, plummeted by nearly two-thirds. Farmers, who Hoover had sought to help, found their crucial overseas markets evaporating.

The act did not cause the Great Depression, but it acted as a powerful poison, transforming a severe national recession into a deeply entrenched global depression. It was a triumph of political short-sightedness over economic sense.

As the months wore on and Hoover's voluntary measures proved woefully inadequate against the tidal wave of bank failures and unemployment, a dark shift occurred in the public mood. The initial shock of the crash turned into a seething, palpable anger. Shantytowns of destitute families on the edges of cities were cruelly dubbed "Hoovervilles." Newspapers used as blankets by the homeless were "Hoover blankets." Empty pockets turned inside out were "Hoover flags." The president's name, once synonymous with efficiency and charity, became a national shorthand for failure and heartless inaction.

Hoover, trapped by his convictions, did eventually approve some federal action, such as the Reconstruction Finance Corporation in 1932 to lend money to banks and railroads. But these steps were hesitant, too limited, and too focused on shoring up institutions rather than feeding people. They were seen as too little, too late—a lifeboat offered after the ship had already sunk.

The growing public fury was no longer just about lost money; it was about broken promises and a government that seemed to watch from a distant shore as its citizens drowned.

The stage was set not for more persuasion, but for revolution at the ballot box.

Chapter 13

From Crash to Depression

The Great Crash of 1929 was a spectacular financial heart attack, but the Great Depression that followed was the long, debilitating illness that nearly ended the patient's life. The stock market collapse did not, by itself, cause the decade-long depression; rather, it was the detonator that set off a chain reaction of economic failures, transforming a severe recession into a catastrophic collapse. The crash shattered the vital nervous system of the American economy: its credit.

The most critical link in this chain was the cascade of bank failures. The banking system, already weakened by its own speculative loans and a fragile structure, was utterly unprepared for the shock. As stock values collapsed, millions of dollars in brokers' loans—the funds that banks had eagerly lent to fuel the speculation—went into default. Simultaneously, terrified depositors, having seen their investments vanish, rushed to withdraw their savings, triggering "runs" on banks.

These runs were a self-fulfilling prophecy; no bank, no matter how sound, could survive if all its depositors demanded their money at once. One by one, then in waves, banks shuttered their doors. Between 1929 and 1933, over nine thousand banks failed, wiping out the life savings of millions of families and vaporizing nearly $7 billion in deposits.

This destruction of capital starved the economy. Businesses that relied on loans for payroll and expansion found the credit taps shut off, forcing them to lay off workers, cut production, or close entirely.

The crash had ignited a fire in the financial sector, and the ensuing bank failures were the explosion that leveled the broader economy.

The conflagration did not stop at the water's edge. The American crisis rapidly became a global contagion. In the 1920s, the United States had been the world's banker, providing crucial loans to war-ravaged European nations, particularly Germany.

After the crash, desperate American banks and investors called in these foreign loans and halted new lending. This withdrawal of American capital plunged Europe into a deep financial crisis. The collapse of world trade, exacerbated by the U.S. Smoot-Hawley Tariff Act, which erected punishing trade barriers, strangled export-driven economies from Latin America to Asia.

As the American economy contracted and demand for imported goods dried up, the global economic engine sputtered and stalled. The world, now intricately connected by finance and trade, was pulled down together. The storm that began on Wall Street had become a global hurricane, leaving a trail of unemployment, poverty, and political instability in its wake.

The Crash was the first domino; the Great Depression was the sound of them all falling.

Chapter 14

The Legacy of Reform

The unrelenting hardship of the Great Depression created a political earthquake, shattering the long-standing Republican dominance of the White House. In 1932, a weary and angry electorate overwhelmingly rejected President Herbert Hoover, whose name had become synonymous with failed promises and breadlines.

In his place, they elected Franklin D. Roosevelt, a man whose patrician confidence and magnetic optimism projected a sense of action and hope that the nation desperately craved. Roosevelt's landslide victory was more than a change of administration; it was a fundamental repudiation of the old order and a mandate for the government to become a direct participant in securing the economic welfare of its citizens.

Roosevelt moved with unprecedented speed, declaring a "New Deal for the American people." In his first hundred days, a whirlwind of legislation was passed, aimed squarely at the root causes of the crash and the ensuing depression.

This new philosophy held that the unregulated, laissez-faire capitalism of the 1920s had proven itself dangerously unstable, and that the federal government had a responsibility to protect the public from the excesses of the financial system.

This philosophy was translated into three landmark reforms that would forever reshape the American financial landscape:

1. **The Federal Deposit Insurance Corporation (FDIC):** Created by the Banking Act of 1933, the FDIC addressed the most visceral fear of the depositor: the loss of their life savings in a bank failure. By insuring bank deposits, the FDIC eliminated the rationale for panic-driven bank runs. The knowledge that their money was safe, even if their bank failed, restored public confidence in the banking system and stopped the destructive cascade of failures at its source.

2. **The Glass-Steagall Act:** This critical piece of legislation erected a firewall within the financial world. It legally separated commercial banking (taking deposits and making loans to individuals and businesses) from investment banking (underwriting securities and speculating in the markets). This prevented banks from gambling with

their depositors' money in the speculative stock market, a key practice that had fueled the bubble and led to catastrophic losses when it burst.

3. **The Securities and Exchange Commission (SEC):** Established in 1934, the SEC was designed to bring transparency and integrity to the stock markets that had been a playground for manipulation and fraud. It required companies selling stock to provide full and truthful disclosure of their financial health, and it enforced laws against insider trading and market manipulation. The SEC was the cop on the beat, tasked with ensuring that the chaotic, rigged casino of the 1920s was transformed into a fair and orderly marketplace.

Together, these reforms represented a profound shift. They acknowledged that the pursuit of profit required guardrails to protect the broader economy and the common citizen.

The legacy of the 1929 crash was not merely one of ruin, but of a hard-won wisdom that was codified into law, creating a more resilient and accountable financial system for generations to come.

Chapter 15

Lessons for the Ages

The story of the 1929 crash is more than a historical account; it is a foundational parable for the modern financial world, its echoes reverberating through every major economic crisis that has followed. While the specific actors and technologies change, the underlying narrative of boom and bust remains hauntingly familiar, revealing enduring truths about markets and human nature.

The parallels with later crises are striking. The **1987 Black Monday** crash shared the same mechanistic, self-reinforcing panic, exacerbated by new technology—in this case, computerized "program trading"—that amplified selling pressure in a way that mirrored the ticker-tape delays of 1929.

The **Dot-com Bubble** of the late 1990s was a near-perfect reenactment of the speculative mania of the 1920s, where "this time is different" thinking justified astronomical valuations for internet companies with no profits, mirroring the blind faith in the "New Era" of radio and aviation.

Most profoundly, the **2008 Global Financial Crisis** served as the most direct echo. It was built on a similarly dizzying pyramid of leverage and opaque financial instruments—collateralized debt obligations (CDOs) instead of investment trusts—and was fueled by a parallel contagion of greed, failed regulation, and a widespread belief that housing prices could never fall.

At the heart of each of these episodes lies the unchanging psychology of the market: the cyclical dance between greed and fear. The 1920s, like every bull market, was driven by an intoxicating greed that silenced caution and rationalized excess.

The crash was the inevitable, violent flip to pure, unadulterated fear. This pattern is a permanent feature of the financial landscape because it is a permanent feature of human nature. The illusion of a "permanently high plateau," whether in stocks, tech, or housing, is a siren song that each new generation seems destined to hear.

The enduring lesson of 1929, therefore, is the critical importance of countervailing forces to this innate instability. **Regulation** is the first and most crucial defense. The reforms of the New Deal—the SEC, FDIC, and Glass-Steagall—were not bureaucratic impediments but vital safeguards born of catastrophe. Their erosion in the decades leading to 2008 demonstrated precisely why they were created. **Transparency** is equally vital; a market cannot function rationally if, as in 1929, investors are buying into complex trusts with no real idea of their underlying assets.

Finally, **financial literacy** serves as a personal line of defense. A populace that understands the basics of leverage, risk, and market cycles is less susceptible to the delusions of a speculative mania.

The Great Crash endures as our most potent cautionary tale. It is a permanent reminder that prosperity built on a foundation of speculation and debt is an illusion, and that the pursuit of wealth without regard for risk contains the seeds of its own destruction.

It teaches that vigilance, not blind faith, is the price of economic stability. The ghosts of October 1929 whisper a warning to every future generation: the music will always stop, and when it does, it is those who understood the rhythm of the dance, not just the euphoria of the party, who will be left standing.

Conclusion

The Crash in Memory

The roar of the trading floor faded, replaced by a silence that settled heavily across the nation. The blizzard of ticker tape was swept away, leaving behind the stark reality of a broken dream. But what became of the souls caught in the storm?

The powerful bankers who had gathered to stem the tide found their influence could not hold back the deluge. Their consortium, a symbol of immense private power, was revealed as a fleeting gesture against a systemic collapse.

While their personal fortunes were bruised, they remained afloat, but their authority was permanently diminished, so to be supplanted by the regulatory state of the New Deal.

The small-time investor, Arthur Miller in his Queens kitchen, faced a harsher fate. His life's savings, invested on a promise of perpetual prosperity, were gone. The new car and his daughter's college fund vanished into the ledger books of a failed brokerage. He joined the ranks of the stunned and the shamed, his faith in the system shattered, his future narrowed to the daily struggle for bread and dignity.

And the floor trader, who had screamed himself hoarse in the heart of the chaos? He became a ghost of the boom, a living relic of a bygone era. Whether he found another trade or succumbed to the despair that claimed so many, he served as a human monument to the day the music stopped—a reminder that the market is not a machine, but a mirror of human nature, reflecting both our boundless optimism and our capacity for blind panic.

The Crash of 1929 did more than wipe out wealth; it fundamentally rewrote the contract between the American people, their government, and the financial system. The age of rugged individualism, of a government that stood aside while fortunes were made and lost, was over.

In its place arose a new consensus: that the state had a vital role to play as a regulator, a protector, and a guarantor of basic economic security. The FDIC would insure savings, the SEC would police the markets, and Social Security would catch the elderly. The relationship was no longer one of hands-off observation but of active, if often awkward, stewardship.

Yet, for all the reforms and the hard-won wisdom, the search for security in the face of economic uncertainty remains one of the defining struggles of the modern world.

The Crash stands as a permanent cautionary tale, a scar on the collective memory warning against the seductive lie of easy money and the folly of believing that risk can be forever banished.

We have built stronger levees, but the ocean of the market remains vast and unpredictable. We have learned to read the weather charts of economics, but we cannot control the climate.

The legacy of Black Tuesday, then, is not just in the laws it inspired, but in the humility it should impose. It is the ghost at the feast of every bull market, the whisper of caution in the ear of every investor, and the sobering reminder that the enduring search for prosperity is, and always will be, a precarious dance on the edge of the unknown.

Appendices

Timeline of Key Events (1929-1933)

1929

- **September 3:** The Dow Jones Industrial Average reaches its pre-crash peak of 381.17.
- **October 24: "Black Thursday."** The first day of panic. A record 12.9 million shares are traded. Major bankers pool funds in a failed attempt to restore confidence.
- **October 28: "Black Monday."** The Dow drops 13%.
- **October 29: "Black Tuesday."** The market completely collapses. A record 16.4 million shares are traded. The ticker tape runs hours behind. Billions of dollars in wealth are obliterated.

- **November 13:** The Dow hits a low for the year of 198.6, a drop of nearly 50% from its September peak.

1930

- **June 17:** The Smoot-Hawley Tariff Act is signed into law, raising U.S. tariffs on thousands of imported goods. This sparks international retaliation and cripples global trade.
- **December:** The Bank of the United States in New York fails, wiping out the accounts of over 400,000 depositors. It is the largest single bank failure in American history to that point and deepens public distrust in the banking system.

1931

- **Spring/Summer:** A wave of bank failures sweeps across the Midwest, accelerating the economic downturn.

- **September:** Great Britain abandons the gold standard, shaking the foundations of the international financial system.
- **The Federal Reserve raises interest rates** to defend the gold standard, a catastrophic decision that worsens the credit crunch and deepens the Depression.

1932

- **January:** The Reconstruction Finance Corporation (RFC) is established to provide emergency government loans to banks, railroads, and other institutions, but its efforts are too limited to stem the tide.
- **Spring:** The Dow hits its ultimate bottom of 41.22, down 89% from its 1929 peak.
- **July:** The "Bonus Army" of World War I veterans is violently dispersed by U.S. Army troops in Washington, D.C., after protesting for early payment of their service bonuses, a event that deeply damages President Hoover's public image.

- **November:** Franklin D. Roosevelt defeats incumbent Herbert Hoover in a landslide presidential election.

1933

- **February:** A new, catastrophic wave of bank runs sweeps the nation, forcing states to declare "bank holidays" to prevent a total collapse.
- **March 4:** Franklin D. Roosevelt is inaugurated, declaring, "The only thing we have to fear is fear itself."
- **March 5:** Roosevelt declares a national "bank holiday," closing all banks to halt the panic.
- **March 9 - June 16: "The Hundred Days."** Roosevelt signs a flurry of New Deal legislation into law, including:
  - The **Emergency Banking Act**, which stabilizes and reopens sound banks.

- The **Glass-Steagall Act**, which establishes the FDIC and separates commercial and investment banking.
- The **Securities Act of 1933**, the first major federal legislation to regulate the stock market.
- **April:** The United States abandons the gold standard.

Glossary of Financial Terms

Blue-Chip Stock

- The stock of a large, well-established, and financially sound company that has a history of reliable performance. In the 1920s, these included companies like U.S. Steel, General Electric, and American Telephone & Telegraph (AT&T). They were considered "safe" investments before the crash.

Broker's Loan

- Money lent to stockbrokers by banks or other lenders, which the brokers then lend to their clients to buy stocks on margin. The massive volume of broker's loans in the late 1920s was a key indicator of dangerous speculation.

Buying on Margin

- The practice of purchasing stocks with borrowed money from a broker. An investor

112

might only put down 10% of the stock's price (the "margin") and borrow the remaining 90%. This magnifies both gains and losses. A small decline in the stock's price could wipe out the investor's entire deposit and trigger a **margin call**.

Dividend

- A portion of a company's profits paid out to its shareholders. During the boom, reliable dividends from utility companies and blue-chip stocks were a major draw for investors.

Federal Reserve (The Fed)

- The central banking system of the United States. Its roles include managing the country's money supply and interest rates. Its failure to curb speculation beforehand and then provide liquidity after the crash was a critical failure.

Investment Trust

- The 1920s predecessor to the modern mutual fund. These companies pooled money from many investors to buy a portfolio of stocks. Many used heavy leverage and complex, opaque structures, which amplified losses during the crash.

Margin Call

- A demand from a broker for an investor to deposit more money or securities to bring their margin account back up to the minimum required value. If the investor cannot meet the call, the broker sells the stock, often at a loss. Widespread margin calls in October 1929 accelerated the market's collapse.

Short Selling (or "Shorting")

- A strategy where an investor borrows shares and immediately sells them, betting that the price will fall. They aim to buy the shares back later at a lower price, return them to the lender, and pocket the difference. While risky, this practice allows investors to profit from a declining market.

Speculation

- The act of conducting a financial transaction with a significant risk of loss, but with the expectation of a substantial gain. Unlike investing, which is focused on the long-term fundamental value of an asset, speculation is often focused on profiting from short-term price fluctuations. The late 1920s market was dominated by speculation.

Stock Ticker

- A telegraph-based machine that printed stock symbols and latest transaction prices on a narrow strip of paper, called ticker tape. On days of heavy trading like Black Tuesday, the ticker fell hours behind, creating massive uncertainty and panic.

Volatility

- The statistical measure of the dispersion of returns for a given security or market index. In simpler terms, it refers to how drastically and rapidly stock prices move up or down. The market became extremely volatile during the crash.

Selected Bibliography and Source Notes

This book is a synthesis of decades of historical scholarship, economic analysis, and firsthand accounts. The following selected works were particularly influential in shaping the narrative and analysis presented in this volume. For the interested reader, they offer avenues for a deeper and more specialized exploration of this pivotal era.

Selected Bibliography

Foundational Histories

- Galbraith, John Kenneth. *The Great Crash, 1929*. Houghton Mifflin, 1954.

  o A classic, witty, and brilliantly accessible economic history that remains a vital starting point for understanding the follies of the era.
- Klein, Maury. *Rainbow's End: The Crash of 1929*. Oxford University Press, 2001.

  o A comprehensive and masterful narrative that situates the crash within the broader social and cultural context of the 1920s.
- Chernow, Ron. *The House of Morgan: An American Banking Dynasty and the Rise of Modern Finance*. Grove Press, 1990.

  o Provides an unparalleled look into the world of high finance and the powerful figures, including the Morgans, who shaped the era.
- Kennedy, David M. *Freedom from Fear: The American People in Depression and

War, 1929-1945*. Oxford University Press, 1999.

- A Pulitzer Prize-winning history that expertly connects the crash to the ensuing Great Depression and the New Deal response.

Specialized Studies and Key Concepts

- Bierman, Harold. *The Causes of the 1929 Stock Market Crash: A Speculative Orgy or a New Era?* Greenwood Press, 1998.

- A focused economic analysis that weighs the various theories behind the crash.
- Pecora, Ferdinand. *Wall Street Under Oath: The Story of Our Modern Money Changers*. Simon and Schuster, 1939.

- The riveting account from the chief counsel of the Senate hearings that exposed the corrupt practices of Wall Street in the years following the crash, directly leading to New Deal reforms.

- Rothbard, Murray N. *America's Great Depression*. Ludwig von Mises Institute, 2000 (5th ed.).

  o A seminal text from the Austrian School of economics, offering a critical interpretation that places primary blame on Federal Reserve policy.

- Shiller, Robert J. *Irrational Exuberance*. Princeton University Press, 2000 (2nd ed., 2005).

  o While focused on later bubbles, Shiller's work on behavioral economics and market psychology provides an essential framework for understanding the herd mentality of the 1920s.

Contemporary Accounts and Broader Context

- Allen, Frederick Lewis. *Only Yesterday: An Informal History of the 1920s*. Harper & Brothers, 1931.

- A vibrant contemporary journalistic history that captures the mood and spirit of the Roaring Twenties as they were experienced.

- Hoover, Herbert. *The Memoirs of Herbert Hoover: The Great Depression, 1929-1941*. Macmillan, 1952.

- President Hoover's own defense of his policies and his perspective on the causes of the Depression.

Source Notes

The narrative in this book is built upon a foundation of primary and secondary sources. Key elements were drawn from the following:

- **Chapter 1 (A New Economic Era):** Statistics on automobile and radio ownership, as well as the philosophy of advertising, are drawn from Klein's *Rainbow's End* and Allen's *Only Yesterday*. The concept of "keeping up with the Joneses" is contextualized using social histories of the period.
- **Chapter 2 (The Engine of the Boom):** The structure of Samuel Insull's utility empire is detailed in Chernow's *The House of Morgan* and business histories of the period. Data on agricultural decline

and income inequality is supported by economic data presented in Kennedy's *Freedom from Fear*.

- **Chapter 3 (Everybody Ought to Be Rich):** John J. Raskob's "Everybody Ought to Be Rich" article was originally published in the *Ladies' Home Journal* (August 1929). The culture of speculation is vividly described in Galbraith's *The Great Crash* and Allen's *Only Yesterday*.
- **Chapter 4 (The Mechanics of Mania):** Explanations of margin buying and brokers' loans are standard in economic histories, with Galbraith providing a particularly clear exposition. The complexity of investment trusts is a key focus in both Galbraith and Pecora.
- **Chapter 5 (Voices of Caution):** The quotes from Roger Babson and Irving Fisher are widely cited in all major histories of the crash, including Galbraith and Klein. Their context and impact are analyzed in these works.
- **Chapters 7 & 8 (The Crash):** The minute-by-minute narrative of Black Thursday and Black Tuesday is compiled from journalistic accounts in *The New York Times* and other contemporary newspapers, synthesized with the dramatic narratives in Klein and Galbraith. The figure of Richard Whitney is prominently featured in Chernow.
- **Chapter 10 (Root Causes):** The "perfect storm" analysis synthesizes the primary theses of Galbraith (speculation), Kennedy (weak fundamentals), and Rothbard (Federal Reserve policy).

- **Chapter 14 (Legacy of Reform):** The details of the New Deal reforms (SEC, FDIC, Glass-Steagall) are drawn from the legislative record and analyzed in Kennedy's *Freedom from Fear*. The political context is further explored in his work and in memoirs of the period.

Printed in Dunstable, United Kingdom